A TRIBUTE TO MOM

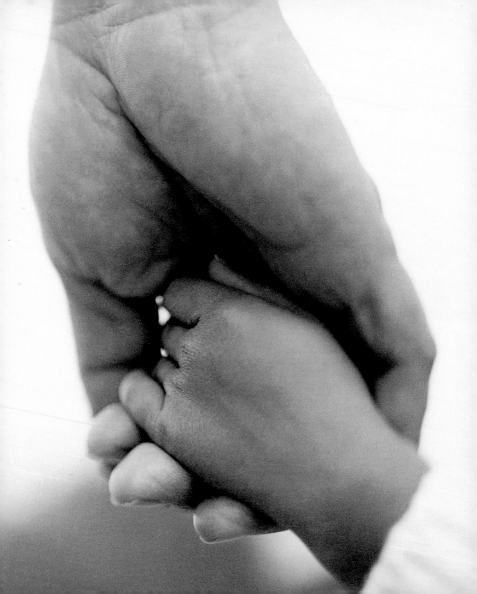

MOTHERS ARE FOREVER

Enduring Bonds of Love

ELLYN SANNA

A DayMaker Greeting Book

For this is the message
that ye heard from the beginning,
that we should love one another.

1 John 3:11 KJV

One of my earliest memories is of my mother singing "Jesus Loves You"—and from my mother's gentle hands I learned what love meant. Because her life taught me the meaning of this word, today I pass love on to my daughter; through me, she catches a glimpse of the God who loves her unconditionally and eternally.

♥

CIRCLES OF LOVE

Mothers of daughters
are daughters of mothers and have remained so,
in circles joined to circles, since time began.
SIGNE HAMMER

ONE HOT DAY LAST SUMMER, MY SEVENTY-
FIVE-YEAR-OLD MOTHER, MY ELEVEN-YEAR-OLD
DAUGHTER, AND I WALKED TOGETHER ACROSS A
SUN-BAKED LAWN. MY MOTHER'S HEART WAS

bothering her, and we walked very slowly, but my daughter didn't mind; she's been complaining that I walk too fast ever since she was small. I listened to their soft voices, watching the way their heads bent toward each other, and I was startled to realize that my daughter is taller than my mother now. My mother said something, and I heard my daughter laugh out loud with delight.

And at that moment, I was suddenly, completely happy. I didn't want to be anywhere but right there, with the

YOUNG WOMAN TO WHOM I HAD GIVEN LIFE,
WITH THE OLDER WOMAN WHO HAD GIVEN ME
LIFE. I THOUGHT OF ANOTHER WOMAN, MY
MOTHER'S MOTHER, NOW IN HEAVEN, AND I
IMAGINED A YOUNG WOMAN YET TO BE BORN,
MY DAUGHTER'S DAUGHTER. TOGETHER WE
FORM A CHAIN OF LOVE REACHING FROM THE
PAST INTO THE FUTURE.

Family faces are magic mirrors.
Looking at people who belong to us,
we see the past, present, and future.

GAIL LUMET BUCKLEY

Heirlooms we don't have

in our family.

But stories we've got.

ROSE CHERNIN

THE RELATIONSHIP BETWEEN A MOTHER AND

HER DAUGHTER IS AS VARIED, AS MYSTERIOUS,

AS CONSTANTLY CHANGING

AND INTERCONNECTED AS

THE PATTERNS THAT TOUCH, MOVE AWAY FROM,

AND TOUCH AGAIN IN A KALEIDOSCOPE.

LYN LIFSHIN

It seems but yesterday you lay new in my arms. . . .
Years slip away—today we are mothers together.
RUTH GRAHAM BELL, *Mothers Together*

WOMEN PASS ON FROM
MOTHER TO DAUGHTER. . .
AT AN EVERYDAY LEVEL OF PRACTICAL CARING
AND AT A DEEPER LEVEL . . . [THIS LEGACY]
IS A TEACHER OF LOVE—THE FIRST TEACHER
AND THE MOST IMPORTANT. . . .
RACHEL BILLINGTON

♥

LESSONS LEARNED

The older women. . .can train the younger women
to love their husbands and children, to be self-controlled
and pure, to be busy at home, to be kind. . . .

TITUS 2:3-5 NIV

IF MY MOTHER HAD BEEN A DIFFERENT WOMAN,
I WOULD BE A DIFFERENT PERSON. WHEN SHE
READ TO ME EACH NIGHT, I LEARNED ABOUT
THE WORLD OF WORDS; TODAY I MAKE MY LIVING

WRITING——AND I STILL LOVE COMING HOME FROM THE LIBRARY WITH A STACK OF BOOKS TO KEEP ME COMPANY. WHEN MY MOTHER TOOK ME OUTDOORS AND NAMED THE TREES AND FLOWERS AND BIRDS FOR ME, I LEARNED ABOUT THE WORLD OF NATURE; TODAY, WHENEVER I'M UPSET OR DISCOURAGED, I STILL FIND PEACE WALKING IN THE WOODS, AND WHEN I RECOGNIZE ASH AND BEECH, TRILLIUMS AND HEPATICA, PURPLE FINCHES AND INDIGO BUNTINGS, I FEEL AS THOUGH I'M SAYING THE NAMES OF DEAR, OLD FRIENDS. AND WHEN MY MOTHER PRAYED WITH ME EACH NIGHT AND

BEFORE EACH MEAL, I LEARNED ABOUT AN ETER-
NAL WORLD; TODAY I SEEK GOD'S PRESENCE
DAILY AND OFFER UP MY LIFE TO HIM IN
PRAYER.

MY MOTHER TRAINED ME WELL.

*Teach your children
to choose the right path,
and when they are older,
they will remain upon it.*

PROVERBS 22:6 NLT

When I stopped seeing mother
with the eyes of a child,
I saw the woman who had helped me
give birth to myself.

NANCY FRIDAY

There is so much to teach,
and the time goes by so fast.

ERMA BOMBECK

In the eyes of its mother
every beetle is a gazelle.

AFRICAN PROVERB

NO MATTER HOW PERFECT

YOUR MOTHER THINKS YOU ARE,

SHE WILL ALWAYS WANT TO FIX YOUR HAIR.

SUZANNE BEILENSON

WHAT DO GIRLS DO

WHO HAVEN'T ANY MOTHERS TO HELP

THEM THROUGH THEIR TROUBLES?

LOUISA MAY ALCOTT

AS DAUGHTERS, WHEN WE SHARE OUR HEARTS

WITH OUR MOTHERS,

WE LEARN FROM THEIR EXPERIENCE.

My Dear Mary,

HOW LONELY THE HOUSE SEEMS —— I NEVER KNEW BEFORE HOW YOU HELPED TO FILL IT. I AM ANXIOUS TO HEAR ABOUT YOUR FIRST IMPRESSIONS OF. . .YOUR NEW HOME. EVER SINCE YOU WENT AWAY, I HAVE BEEN WONDERING IF IT WAS AS HARD FOR YOU TO GO OUT INTO THE WORLD AS IT WAS FOR ME TO HAVE YOU GO.

DON'T WRITE SHORT, HURRIED LETTERS, SIMPLY STATING FACTS IN THEIR TERSEST FORM, BUT TELL ME ALL YOUR THOUGHTS AND DREAMS AND PLANS, YOUR WORRIES AND TRIALS, AND WE WILL TALK THEM OVER AS TWO COMRADES. . . . IF

THERE IS ANYTHING IN MY LIFE THAT CAN BE OF
VALUE TO YOU, I WANT YOU TO HAVE IT; IF I CAN
SAVE YOU A STUMBLE OR A SINGLE FALSE STEP, I
WANT TO DO IT, BUT THE ONLY WAY I CAN DO IT IS
TO KNOW YOUR HEART.

Your loving mother.
Florence Wenderoth Saunders

THE ART OF MOTHERING

IS HANDED DOWN

FROM ONE GENERATION

TO THE NEXT.

WENDY JEAN RUHL

WHENEVER I FEEL MYSELF INFERIOR TO EVERYTHING ABOUT ME. . .I CAN STILL HOLD UP MY HEAD AND SAY TO MYSELF: I AM THE DAUGHTER OF THE WOMAN WHO. . .AT THE AGE OF SEVENTY-SIX WAS PLANNING JOURNEYS AND UNDERTAKING THEM. . . .

I AM THE DAUGHTER OF A WOMAN WHO, IN A MEAN, CLOSE-FISTED, CONFINED LITTLE PLACE, OPENED HER VILLAGE HOUSE TO STRAY CATS, TRAMPS, AND PREGNANT SERVANT-GIRLS. I AM THE DAUGHTER OF A WOMAN WHO MANY TIMES, WHEN SHE WAS IN DESPAIR AT NOT HAV- ING ENOUGH MONEY FOR OTHERS, RAN THROUGH THE WIND-WHIPPED SNOW TO CRY

FROM DOOR TO DOOR, AT THE HOUSES OF THE RICH, THAT A CHILD HAD JUST BEEN BORN IN A POVERTY-STRICKEN HOME TO PARENTS WHOSE FEEBLE, EMPTY HANDS HAD NO SWADDLING CLOTHES FOR IT.

LET ME NOT FORGET: I AM THE DAUGHTER OF A WOMAN WHO BENT HER HEAD, TREMBLING, BETWEEN THE BLADES OF A CACTUS, HER WRINKLED FACE FULL OF ECSTASY OVER THE PROMISE OF A FLOWER, A WOMAN WHO HERSELF NEVER CEASED TO FLOWER, UNTIRINGLY, DURING THREE QUARTERS OF A CENTURY.

COLETTE

The thing about mothers is. . .

You can't lie when you're looking into their eyes.

When they're on a diet, everyone in the family has to be on a diet, too.

All their daughters are geniuses.

They are each and every one the best cook in the whole world.

They always take your side in an argument——unless you're arguing with them.

No matter how old you get, they're the best people to have around when you're sick.

The thing about daughters is. . .

Even when they're not with you, you can never escape their presence in your heart.

They need love most when they're hardest to love.

Once they're teenagers, no matter how much they love you, they're still embarrassed by you.

They are so much like you, yet so different.

They can break your heart one moment and make you laugh with joy the next.

They often steal your clothes from your closet and yet will never listen to your advice when the two of you shop for clothes.

We not only learn from our mothers, though. As a mother, I learn something new from my daughters almost every day.

The moment my oldest daughter was born, I was awestruck that God could have loved me so much that He would entrust into my care this perfect, beautiful little person.

And as she grew older, I learned to play again, to laugh out loud at silly things. I learned that children's books are as good as grown-up volumes, and I learned that playing in the creek is still as much fun as it was when I was small. When I did the laundry, my daughter would stand on a chair beside me,

WATCHING THE SWIRLING CLOTHES IN THE WASHING MACHINE, AND I LEARNED THAT EVEN ORDINARY CHORES ARE FULL OF JOY.

As I write this, I look out my window and see my daughter walking toward me, home from school. She's no longer very excited about the laundry—but as she comes through the door, her smile delights me as much as it did when I would pick her up out of her crib after a nap. And the love she gives me, the daily forgiveness she grants me when I'm impatient, the understanding she extends when I'm discouraged, all these things teach me that God's love for me is still both awesome and full of joy.

My daughter introduced me to the soothing luxury of a bubble bath and to the charms of reading out loud and pretending. Her expressiveness has encouraged my own.

I find the edges of my personality rounding out. . . .

Angela McBride

♥

In sharing your childhood discoveries,

I have relived my own.

♥

LETTING GO

A mother is not a person to lean on .
but a person to make leaning unnecessary.

DOROTHY CANFIELD FISHER

AS DAUGHTERS, IT'S HARD TO LET GO OF OUR

MOTHERS. NO MATTER HOW OLD WE ARE, WE CAN

STILL HEAR THEIR VOICES IN OUR HEADS. BUT

AS MUCH AS WE LOVE THEM, AS MUCH AS THEY

LOVE US, GOD WANTS HIS VOICE TO BE LOUDER THAN OUR MOTHERS'. AS MOTHERS, IT'S HARD TO LET GO OF OUR DAUGHTERS. WE WOULD LIKE TO BE WITH THEM WHEREVER THEY GO IN LIFE, PROTECTING THEM FROM ALL LIFE'S DANGERS. BUT GOD WANTS US TO PUT OUR DAUGHTERS IN HIS HANDS, TRUSTING THAT HIS LOVE WILL PROVIDE FOR THEM FAR BETTER THAN WE EVER COULD.

I love my daughter. She and I have shared my body.
There is a part of her mind that is part of mine.
But when she was born, she sprang from me like a slippery fish,
and has been swimming away ever since.

AMY TAN

It's like a magnet,

the mother-daughter relationship.

One day, your daughter

clings for dear life;

the next, she's pushing you away.

KAREN PHILLIPS

[MY] GIRLS AREN'T SOMETHING I CREATED;

I FEEL LIKE I RECEIVED THE HONOR OF

BEING THE VEHICLE FOR BRINGING THESE

SOULS INTO THE WORLD. . . . BUT I DON'T MAKE

THE MISTAKE OF THINKING I OWN THEM.

ROSANNE CASH

Sometimes the best way to let go is by forgiving. . .

My first-grade daughter is still convinced I'm the most beautiful woman in the world. But a few mornings ago my sixth-grader was embarrassed by my appearance.

She was already around the corner, waiting for the school bus, when I noticed her lunch left on the kitchen table. Without thinking twice, I grabbed it up, and dressed in my sweats, my hair still rumpled from my pillow, I dashed down the sidewalk, my old moccasins slipping and sliding on my feet. "Emily!" I shouted. "You forgot your lunch."

She threw a horrified look at me, and

HER EYES FILLED WITH TEARS. THE OTHER KIDS WAITING AT THE BUS STOP WHISPERED AND GIGGLED TO EACH OTHER. I GLANCED FROM THEM TO MY DAUGHTER, AND SUDDENLY I REALIZED THAT I HARDLY LOOKED MY BEST. AND I REMEMBERED ONCE MORE WHAT IT FELT LIKE TO BE THAT AGE, WHEN EACH SMALL DISCREPANCY IN A PERSON'S APPEARANCE WAS FAIR GAME FOR RIDICULE.

WHO CARES? I WANTED TO TELL HER. DON'T LET YOURSELF BE AS PETTY AS THEY ARE. DO YOU THINK I CARE WHAT A BUNCH OF TWELVE-YEAR-OLDS THINKS OF ME?

BUT I CARED WHAT SHE THOUGHT OF ME. AND IT HURT TO KNOW THAT FOR THE FIRST TIME IN HER LIFE, SHE WAS ASHAMED OF ME.

That day after school, she and I were especially nice to each other. I knew she had forgiven me for embarrassing her. And I forgave her for no longer thinking I was the most beautiful and perfect woman in the world. I guess I was really forgiving her for growing up.

There is no influence so powerful
as that of the mother.
Sarah Josepha Hale

♥

Raising daughters is like mountain climbing. . .

you can't keep them from taking chances in

life. They're going to leave no matter what——

it's making sure you've used the right rope

and given the right amount of slack.

Eileen Brown

ONE OF THE MOST VALUABLE LESSONS
I LEARNED. . .IS THAT WE ALL HAVE TO LEARN
FROM OUR MISTAKES AND WE LEARN FROM
THOSE MISTAKES A LOT MORE THAN
WE LEARN FROM THE THINGS WE SUCCEEDED
IN DOING. I HAVE TO GIVE MY. . .
DAUGHTERS THE OPPORTUNITY
TO MAKE MISTAKES.

ANN RICHARDS

I looked at this rolled-up bundle. . .
and knew again I had not created her. She was herself
apart from me. She had her own life to lead, her own destiny
to accomplish; she just came past me to this earth.
My job was to get her to adulthood and push her off.

KATHARINE TREVELYAN

♥

Our goal is to steadily turn our
[daughters] away from their earthly
parents, who will let them down,
toward a heavenly Father who will always
be there for them and in whose arms
they will always be secure.

Susan Alexander Yates

♥

Hearts Entwined Forever

*Your relationship with your daughters
is one you can rely on, there for life,
an ongoing, developing relationship.*

Enid Johns

When my daughter Emily was little, she was
my constant companion. Her little chatter-
ing voice brought new life to everything
I did, from family visits to grocery shopping,

FROM TRIPS TO THE BANK TO WALKS IN THE WOODS.

Once, waiting in an examination room for my doctor, the two of us were talking a blue streak when the nurse came in.

"You two are best buddies, aren't you?" she said. And we were.

When Emily went to preschool for the first time, I gave her a gold heart of mine to wear, to remind her that my love went with her. When I went into the hospital for the birth of my second child, she gave it back to remind me that her love would be with me. And when she went to kindergarten, I bought her a duplicate

NECKLACE, SO THAT SHE WOULD KNOW SHE WAS ALWAYS IN MY HEART.

But as she grew older and my life got busier, filled now with two more children and the responsibilities of my career, I sometimes worried that I would lose her, that she would disappear into her own new world of school and friends, and I would never recover the person who had been such a good companion to me.

But lately, as she becomes a young woman instead of a child, I find we relate to each other a in new way. Now, as we lie on my big bed and have woman-to-woman talks, I realize she's still a good companion. And yesterday, as she was hurrying off to meet her friends, I noticed the small gold heart that glittered at her throat. I touched the gold heart around my own neck and smiled.

The daughter never gives up on the mother,
just as the mother never gives up on the daughter.
There is a tie here so strong nothing can break it.

RACHEL BILLINGTON

It's my belief that between mothers and daughters
there is a kind of blood-hyphen that is,
finally, indissoluble.

CAROL SHIELDS

ONCE A MOTHER, ALWAYS A MOTHER—

EVEN IF YOUR DAUGHTER IS SEVENTY.

THE RELATIONSHIP CHANGES, OF COURSE,

BUT IS NO LESS IMPORTANT.

RACHEL BILLINGTON

A DAUGHTER AND HER MOTHER ARE
NEVER FREE OF ANOTHER. . . . FOR THEY ARE
SO ENTWINED IN HEART AND MIND THAT . . .
THEY SHARE EACH LOVE, EACH JOY, EACH SORROW
AND EACH BITTER WRONG LIFE-LONG.

PAM BROWN

A woman should always stand by a woman.

EURIPIDES

HOW VAST A MEMORY HAS LOVE!

ALEXANDER POPE

There is nothing Madison Avenue can give us
that will make us more beautiful women.
We are beautiful because God created us that way.

MARIANNE WILLIAMSON

OUR DAUGHTERS ARE THE MOST PRECIOUS

OF OUR TREASURES, AND THE DEAREST

POSSESSIONS OF OUR HOMES, AND THE

OBJECTS OF OUR MOST WATCHFUL LOVE.

MARGARET E. SANGSTER

Keep your face to the sunshine
and you cannot see the shadow.

HELEN KELLER

♥

Looking Ahead

And all thy children shall be taught of the Lord;
and great shall be the peace of thy children.

Isaiah 54:13 KJV

My mother still worries about me. She longs for my happiness and well-being, and I suspect my illnesses are far harder on her than they are on me. I know her prayers go with me wherever I go.

As my own daughters grow up, I know that I, too, will worry about them until the day I die. I cannot protect them from all pain. But my prayer for them is that they will be strong in Christ Jesus, that in Him they will find their peace. He will still be with them when I am gone. And I can trust their growing-up years, their adulthood, their old age, and even their deaths to Him.

FLOWERS GROW OUT OF DARK MOMENTS.

CORITA KENT

Thank You, God, for the gift of my mother.

Bless her, please, with Your love and kindness.

May she always walk with You.

And, God, thank You for my daughter.

Care for her, watch over her,

lead her in paths of truth.

May she always know You are with her.

Thank You, Lord, for creating

both of these wonderful women.

I am so grateful for mothers and daughters!

Amen

A KINDHEARTED WOMAN GAINS RESPECT.

PROVERBS 11:16 NIV

She wore age so gracefully, so carelessly,
that there was a sacred beauty about her faded cheek
more lovely and lovable than all the bloom of her youth.
Happy woman who was not afraid of growing old.

DINAH MARIA MULOCK

YOUR BEAUTY. . .SHOULD BE THAT OF YOUR

INNER SELF, THE UNFADING BEAUTY

OF A GENTLE AND QUIET SPIRIT, WHICH

IS OF GREAT WORTH IN GOD'S SIGHT.

1 PETER 3:3-4 NIV

If you have made mistakes,

even serious ones,

there is always another chance for you.

What we call failure is not the falling down,

but the staying down.

MARY PICKFORD

Never grow a wishbone, daughter,

where your backbone ought to be.

CLEMENTINE PADDLEFORD

No one can make you feel inferior

without your consent.

ELEANOR ROOSEVELT

© 2003 by Barbour Publishing, Inc.

ISBN 1-58660-814-2

Photo Credits: Cover and page six, Mel Klein /Photonica ; page 20, Workbookstock;
page 30, Steven Puetzer /Photonica ; page 40, Ellen Denuto /Photonica ; page 51, Gary Isaacs /Photonica;
book design by Kevin Keller /designconcept;

Scripture quotations marked KJV are taken from
the King James Version of the Bible.
Scripture quotations marked NLT are taken from the Holy Bible,
New Living Translation, copyright© 1996. Used by permission of
Tyndale House Publishers, Inc., Wheaton, Illinois 60189, U.S.A. All rights reserved.
Scripture quotations marked NIV are taken from the Holy Bible, New International Version ®,
NIV ®. Copyright © 1973, 1978, 1984 by International Bible Society.
Used by permission of Zondervan Publishing House. All rights reserved.

Published by Barbour Publishing, Inc., P. O. Box 719, Uhrichsville, Ohio44683,
www.barbourbooks.com.

Member of the
Evangelical Christian
Publishers Association

Printed in China

5 4 3 2